Bitcoin Decoded

BRETT COMBS

and

TOM MITSOFF

BRETT COMBS and TOM MITSOFF

DEDICATIONS

I dedicate this book to my mother Ruth and my late father, Chris, who experienced more peaks and valleys in life than any good couple should ever have to deal with. But along the way, they always put me and my siblings Christine, Lee and David as their top priority. They should be so very proud of the lives they have lived and helped to shape.

— Tom Mitsoff, co-author

I dedicate this took to my loving family. Friends come and go through the ups and downs in life, but I've always been able to count on my family. Blood does indeed form thick bonds. Thank you Mom, Dad, Dustin (Bro), Debbie and Alex (Gadget) in spite of it all. I love you all and you mean the world to me.

— Brett Combs, co-author

CONTENTS

Disclaimer

This material has been prepared by Propellerhead Marketing. This book is for information and illustrative purposes only and does not purport to show actual results. It is not, and should not be regarded as investment advice or as a recommendation regarding any particular security or course of action. Opinions expressed herein are current opinions as of the date appearing in this material only and are subject to change without notice. Reasonable people may disagree about the opinions expressed herein. In the event any of the assumptions used herein do not prove to be true, results are likely to vary substantially. All investments entail risks. There is no guarantee that investment strategies will achieve the desired results under all market conditions and each investor should evaluate its ability to invest for a long term especially during periods of a market downturn. No representation is being made that any account, product, or strategy will or is likely to achieve profits, losses, or results similar to those discussed, if any. No part of this document may be reproduced in any manner, in whole or in part, without the prior written permission of Propellerhead Marketing Group, LLC.

This information is provided with the understanding that with respect to the material provided herein, that you will make your own independent decision with respect to any course of action in connection herewith and as to whether such course of action is appropriate or proper based on your own judgment, and that you are capable of understanding and assessing the merits of a course of action.

Propellerhead Marketing Group, LLC shall not have any liability for any damages of any kind whatsoever relating to this material. You should consult your advisors with respect to these areas. By continuing to read this material, you acknowledge, understand and accept the foregoing.

Preface

We are simply amazed at the progress Bitcoin has made in the few short years since we released the first edition of this book in 2014. What started out for us as a desire to teach others about Bitcoin has turned into an amazing journey.

In releasing the third version (second revision) of the book, we listened to our readers' feedback. We have created a "Quick Start" chapter since so many of you simply want to get started buying your first Bitcoin. We also reduced the number of web links that were a distraction, leaving only what we felt were important. Finally, we revised some sections and removed others that we felt were not relevant to our mission of teaching you the basics of cryptocurrencies and Bitcoin.

We hope you enjoy the revisions and would love to hear from you if you have comments or questions:

info@bitcoincoaches.com
www.bitcoincoaches.com

Brett Combs and Tom Mitsoff

Introduction

In 2009, a Norwegian named Kristoffer Koch purchased 5,000 Bitcoins for 150 Norwegian Kroner (or about $26 USD) as part of his work on a research thesis on encryption on which he was working. After that, he forgot all about his purchase until early in 2013 when Bitcoin was getting a lot of media buzz. By the time he decided to exchange his Bitcoins for currency, they were worth about $21 million USD[1].

In 2010, Floridian Laszlo Hanyecz thought it would be "interesting" to be able to say he paid for a pizza in Bitcoins. He worked out a deal where he transferred 10,000 of his Bitcoins to another guy, who ordered him two pizzas from Papa John's. Today, those 10,000 Bitcoins would be worth about $42 million. So Mr. Hanyecz has a humorous story about the pizza that cost him $42 million.

This book will give you an understanding of how something you can't hold in your hands has become extremely valuable.[2] Based on our years of experience dealing with Bitcoin we will steer you toward your best opportunities to, perhaps, be one of the next Kristoffer Koch stories.

---

[1] At the time we are editing this version of the Bitcoin Decoded book, Bitcoin is trading at $4,200 USD.

[2] Currently Bitcoin is trading over three times the value of an an ounce of gold!

As you begin to read this book either in digital ink or in print, there are a lot of unknowns and much confusion surrounding Bitcoin -- something which you may not have heard about until recently.

Very likely, the reason you have chosen to purchase and read this book is you have heard the buzz about Bitcoin in the media or from friends or co-workers, and you are curious but you don't really understand much more than its name.

Our objectives in writing this book are to help you understand what Bitcoin is, and bring understanding to the complexities in the way it is created and functions. It is absolutely critical you understand how and why it exists, as well as some of the potential pitfalls, before you dive in.

Currently, you need a fairly high level of understanding and expertise to swim safely in the Bitcoin pool. This book is the equivalent of the swimming lessons you took as a kid in the shallow end of the pool. Once you've finished the book, you'll be able to go into the water safely, and be aware of both the potential dangers and thrills of the deep end of the metaphorical Bitcoin pool. This book is your lifeguard -- follow its directions to stay safe.

Most importantly, once you've finished this book, you will be up to speed on the basics of Bitcoin, and you'll be able to safely explore what your place in the Bitcoin ecosystem might be.

We invite you to journey with us and continue reading.

1 Quick Start:
Buy Bitcoin in 4 Easy Steps

Upon starting the second revision (third version) of this book, the authors realized that many of their readers wanted to get started quickly in buying their first Bitcoin without having to read the entire book. This chapter was added to help you make your first purchase with Bitcoin without any prior knowledge or understanding. Subsequent chapters go into greater detail explaining what Bitcoin is. So if you are ready to buy Bitcoin, let's get started.

There are four steps you will need to complete to purchase Bitcoin, and then to receive Bitcoin and send it to others.

Step 1. What is Bitcoin?

Bitcoin is a new form of currency, an Internet currency (also known as cryptocurrency). It allows one person to send another person payments directly. The payments do not go through a third party (ie., PayPal, a bank, or a traditional merchant network). Bitcoin exists only on the Internet. Without the Internet, there would be no Bitcoin. Bitcoin derives its value through the market forces of supply and demand. The collective actions of the marketplace are what create its value.

Step 2. Get Yourself a Bitcoin Address

Bitcoin payments operate like bank transfers. Each person has his or her own private "account," which is called a Bitcoin address. A Bitcoin address is 26 to 35 alphanumeric characters beginning with the number 1 or 3. This address represents a destination for a Bitcoin payment. A person possessing an address can receive Bitcoin in any amount from another person anywhere on the planet, even in outer space, in seconds. A person can have multiple addresses that are stored together in an electronic version of a wallet, called a digital wallet.

The authors highly recommend using the USA-based company, Coinbase. Coinbase has been in operation since 2012 and has a fantastic track record in exchanging digital assets like Bitcoin securely and without any major hassles. Located in San Francisco, Coinbase exchanges fiat currencies (i.e., U.S. dollar) in 32 countries and facilitates Bitcoin transactions and storage in 190 countries worldwide. The authors have no financial interest or gain in recommending the company. There are other wallets you could use, simply Google "bitcoin wallet".[3]

You can set up your account at Coinbase: www.coinbase.com

Setting up an account with Coinbase is fairly easy. As part of the process of setting up your account and removing deposit and spending limits, you'll need to complete an identity verification

---

[3] Beware of using a wallet or exchange service that does not have a vettable track record, as you can lose your Bitcoin to a breach or hack. One of the authors experienced this early in his Bitcoin ventures.

process. The process is no more difficult than opening a bank account here in the USA.

Coinbase starts you off with several different wallets. For the purpose of buying your first Bitcoin, you'll focus on the default Bitcoin wallet.

With your address and wallet setup, you are ready to move to Step 3.

Step 3. Buy Bitcoin

Using Coinbase or another digital asset exchange, you'll purchase Bitcoin by using your debit / credit card, or a bank or wire transfer of your fiat currency[4] (i.e., U.S. dollar). Then, Coinbase will convert your fiat currency to Bitcoin for a small fee. Bitcoin is divisible up to 8 decimal places, so you do not have to buy a whole Bitcoin. You can buy small fractional amounts that correspond to your fiat currency budget.

Here is an example of a way to buy Bitcoin on even a very small budget, and how it can appreciate in value quickly.

From June through August 2017, we set up an automated buy of Bitcoin through Coinbase every two weeks. On each occasion, we spent $16.67 in U.S. dollars, and each time, it bought a slightly different amount of Bitcoin, due to the cryptocurrency's volatility. Each purchase included a small fee for Coinbase, and ended up at $16.91.

The five purchases totalling $84.55 brought .031869 Bitcoin into our Coinbase Bitcoin wallet. Just a few weeks later on August 21,

---

[4] Fiat Currency is discussed in Chapter 5.

2017, that Bitcoin purchased for $84.55 had a value of $124.70, or a 47 percent increase in a short period of time.

Please note, this is not a guarantee of asset appreciation. You should study the history of Bitcoin's value and make your own decision. The primary points of this example are that you can purchase fractions of Bitcoin and experience the same potential for appreciation as individuals who own whole Bitcoins. Cryptocurrencies are not only for the wealthy. Anyone can get involved, as the example above illustrates.

If you decide not to use Coinbase, the steps to buy Bitcoin are different for each exchange. Simply follow the process created by each exchange.

Some Bitcoin purchases are instant with Coinbase. If you have gone through simple identify verification and linked a debit/credit card with Coinbase, purchase show up in your digital wallet in seconds. Bank transfers generally take five to seven days before you have access to your Bitcoin. You lock in your conversion price the moment you make the purchase, which could work to your advantage in a rising Bitcoin market or a disadvantage if Bitcoin price decreases.

Given Bitcoin's current volatility, if you are buying a service or product with Bitcoin based upon a fiat price (i.e., pricing the item or service in U.S. dollars), you might need more or less Bitcoin for the transaction, depending on the moment in time. It's always good to have extra Bitcoin to take care of price movement if you are paying for thing based on fiat value.

Step 4. Make a Payment

Remember your Bitcoin address from Step 1? To make a payment to someone else, you'll need his or her unique Bitcoin address. Then you'll need to know how much you need to pay. Assuming you have funds in your Bitcoin wallet, you are ready to send payment.

It might be as easy as sending .0013000 Bitcoin to 1MauqJEVKx7mohEXXaHXnn96RFvLEGnVjV, or a bit more complicated, as sending 123.12345678 Bitcoins to 1MauqJEVKx7mohEXXaHXnn96RFvLEGnVjV. As you most likely will be doing this on your computer, it is a much better idea to just copy and paste the destination address instead of trying to type it in.[5]

Go to Coinbase or other Bitcoin wallet provider, and find the location where you can input your recipient's Bitcoin address and amount and send the payment.

We highly recommend copy/pasting information like the payment address with the final step of triple-confirming the Bitcoin address you are sending to. One typo could result in entering an incorrect Bitcoin address, and your Bitcoin being sent to some unknown wallet. If that happens, you can kiss it goodbye. There is no way to recover it.

We have oversimplified the process here. But if you use Coinbase, it is very easy to set up everything properly with the basic instructions outlined here. You should be able to send Bitcoin reliably and quickly.

Now let's move on to learning what Bitcoin is, its past and its future.

---

[5] Don't send anything to that Bitcoin address as it is used for illustration purposes.

2 What is Bitcoin?

For the vast majority of people, Bitcoin is a revolutionary idea that doesn't fit well into their current understanding of monetary systems, trade, commerce and computing. Bitcoin uses odd terms such as cryptocurrencies, digital money, consensus networks, peer-to-peer technology and decentralized control – terms that tend to evoke confusion, fear and skepticism for many. The authors do not see Bitcoin as revolutionary. Bitcoin is really evolutionary and creates a monetary and payment system built for the online realm.

The objective of this book is to demystify Bitcoin and provide you solid footing for you to form your own opinions. Here are the basics, which are important to understand before we dive deeper into the subject.

Bitcoin Defined?

Bitcoin is digital money that can be spent or traded with anyone else in the world willing to accept it from you. You don't need to exchange your Bitcoins for dollars, pounds, pesos, francs or any other local currency, as long as the person or business you are trading with is willing to accept Bitcoins and has the ability to receive them with a Bitcoin wallet.

Bitcoin was the very first of the growing number of cryptocurrencies, which exist on and because of the Internet. Without the Internet, Bitcoin and other cryptocurrencies would not exist.

Cryptocurrencies are digital money and based on the principles of cryptography and mathematics. Cryptography is the practice of securing communication between two parties in the presence of a third party, potentially adversarial. Modern applications using cryptography include ATM cards, computer passwords and, of course, secure web commerce.

Cryptography prior to the modern age was effectively synonymous with encryption, the conversion of information from a readable state to apparent nonsense. The beauty of the apparent nonsense is it can be converted back to meaningful information with the right keys. In the case of cryptocurrencies, the information in digital wallets[6] and the payment data traveling on the network is encrypted.

---

[6] Not all digital wallets are secured with encryption by default. To protect cryptocurrencies, the reader should make sure his/her digital wallet is encrypted and protected with a strong password before storing currency in the digital wallet. Digital wallets and wallet security are discussed later in the book.

The integrity of Bitcoin and all other cryptocurrencies is enforced with cryptography, using the ingenious and proven methods found in public key encryption systems.

The mathematical aspects of cryptocurrencies are quite complex and beyond the scope of an introductory book on Bitcoin. But suffice it to say, mathematics are at the core of cryptocurrencies as they are used as an economic measure to deter abuses which will be discussed in another chapter.

With our basic definition in place, let's go a little deeper. Let's go right to the source, which is Bitcoin.org. Here's what the Bitcoin.org website says:

"Bitcoin is a consensus network that enables a new payment system and a completely digital money. It is the first decentralized peer-to-peer payment network that is powered by its users with no central authority or middlemen. From a user perspective, Bitcoin is pretty much like cash for the Internet. Bitcoin can also be seen as the most prominent triple-entry bookkeeping system in existence."

Since that explanation is full of geekspeak, let's break Bitcoin.org's definition into pieces:

1. "Consensus network:" This is a network of computers working together to solve the same problem or goal. In the case of Bitcoin, the consensus network is made up of computers around the globe running mining software. The goal of the network is confirming or validating transactions. Mining will be discussed at greater length later in the book.

2. "Completely digital money:" You can't touch or hold Bitcoin. It's virtual. Think of it as you would currency in

your regular bank account if you could only check it through your online banking interface, and only receive or spend through your computer or smartphone.

3.   "Peer-to-peer payment network:" Bitcoin protocol operates on the Internet through direct interactions between software running on tens of thousands of interconnected computers around the globe. The network is known as a "distributed consensus system," in Bitcoin-speak. The system is used to confirm transactions and include them into the network's public ledger.

4.   "No central authority or middlemen:" As mentioned above, there are no banks between you and the person with whom you are trading Bitcoin. The benefits include near-instantaneous payment and receipt of money with no large fees extracted from payment processors -- like you would pay if you use credit cards or other payment networks. A small fee of .0001 Bitcoin is charged to the sender under special circumstances. That equates to around 40 cents USD, much less than the amounts charged by most ATMs and money exchangers like Western Union.

5.   "Triple-entry bookkeeping system:" In simplest terms, this means when two parties agree to a transaction, a third party also agrees to confirm it. In the case of Bitcoin, the third party is other interconnected computers in the consensus network that validate and confirm the transaction. Each transaction is validated by numerous computers in the network before it is considered valid and is stored for public inspection. The process of confirmation creates trust between the parties sending and receiving payments. Creating trust is

at the core of all monetary systems, and the bookkeeping system used creates that trust.

How is Bitcoin Created?

Again, from Bitcoin.org:

"New Bitcoins are generated by a competitive and decentralized process called 'mining.' This process involves that individuals are rewarded by the network for their services. Bitcoin miners are processing transactions and securing the network using specialized hardware and are collecting new Bitcoins in exchange."

Exactly what is Bitcoin mining? It could be more accurately described as competitive and completely digital bookkeeping. Miners use high-powered devices to build and maintain a gigantic digital public ledger. This ledger is called the blockchain. The blockchain contains a record of every Bitcoin transaction in its history. It is rumored the Bitcoin public ledger is the world's largest shared public ledger. Considering it consists only of past Bitcoin transactions, the size of the blockchain is staggering.

Every time Bitcoins are sent, the transaction has to be validated by computers around the globe running the mining software. The software checks the ledger to make sure the sender transferring Bitcoin actually possesses it. This process is known as confirmation.

If the transaction proves to be valid, the Bitcoin protocol adds it to the blockchain. The Bitcoin network rewards the miner with Bitcoins for work performed to validate the transaction.

More accurately, only one miner is rewarded for each block.[7] Miners are all competing with each other to be first to solve a complex math problem which is packing up transactions to form a new block.

With each fresh block, the winner takes all of the Bitcoins awarded for that block.[8] However, as we will discuss in more detail later, many people mining now are doing so as part of groups called mining pools. When one of those mining pools solves a block, members of that pool share the reward. As mining operations and pools grow, it is not at all unusual for a miner participating in that pool to receive a tiny fraction of a Bitcoin as each block is solved. It is important to note rewards paid to miners are the only way new Bitcoins are introduced or created.[9]

Mining is a rather ingenious process. How can you incentivize individuals to devote computing power and electricity to validate transactions and solve blocks? Reward them with Bitcoin! Those who started mining when Bitcoin had no value and have held their Bitcoins are some of today's Internet millionaires.

What Gives Bitcoin its Value?

In simplest terms, what gives Bitcoin its value is people's desire to acquire it, hold it, and use it to buy and sell things.

---

[7] Data is permanently recorded in the blockchain (transaction ledger) through digital records called blocks. A block is a record of some or all the most recent Bitcoin transactions that have not been recorded in any prior blocks.

[8] The reward halves at a predetermined rate and the reward will eventually be zero (0). Then no more coins will likely be created.

[9] So what happens when all coins are mined? According to current estimates, it could take until the year 2040. Financial incentive to keep miners mining should exist for at least a couple more decades.

Throughout history, people have found clever ways to use the technology of their age to create easier ways to transact commerce. Bitcoin is just the most efficient way to transact commerce in an increasingly digital world.

Cue Bitcoin.org:

"Bitcoins have value because they are useful as a form of money. Bitcoin has the characteristics of money (durability, portability, fungibility, scarcity, divisibility, and recognizability) based on the properties of mathematics rather than relying on physical properties (like gold and silver) or trust in central authorities (like fiat currencies)."

What is Money?

Money is officially issued currency and coin. Governments define the medium of exchange used in their respective economies. Money is often thought of as cash, but also includes other negotiable instruments like checks.

Each country has its own money, and some countries share a type of currency like the Euro, which is used by the European Union. Money and currencies are synonymous, and modern currency systems use fiat currency.

What is Fiat Currency?

Fiat is Latin meaning "let it be done," "it shall be." Fiat currency is the term used to describe the currency used in a country or group of countries. The first fiat monies were thought to originate from China about 1,000 years ago.

In the last thousand years, some countries have used fiat currencies normally backed with gold and silver. The money itself might not be gold or silver, or made from gold or silver, but there was gold and/or silver in a country's treasury to back or assure the holder of fiat that their money was worth something and could be converted to gold or silver.

After World War II, the Bretton Woods Accord set up a system whereby currency supplies were pegged to the U.S. dollar and then the U.S. dollar was pegged to gold (known as the gold standard).

In 1971, United States President Richard Nixon shocked the world by moving the U.S. dollar off the gold standard and ended the U.S. dollar's ability to be converted to gold. Since 1971, all currencies have been fiat currencies.

Now the value of any fiat currency is controlled, for better or worse, by monetary policy and not the price of gold or silver. No country now uses the gold standard as the basis of its monetary system. The movement away of from a gold standard allows countries to deficit- or debt-finance their economies.

Fiat currencies are declared by a government to be legal tender. This means it must be accepted as a form of payment if offered. Fiat currencies are generally paper or minted metal. Fiat currencies have value because an issuing government says they have value.

The piece of paper on which a United States $20 bill is printed upon is not worth $20 until the United States Mint runs it through its elaborate printing, trimming and distribution processes. It is then introduced to the money supply by the Federal Reserve Bank through its member banks to your local bank (if you live in the United States). If you live outside the U.S., the entity or regulating body in your country is involved in a similar process.

Although the $20 bill is not backed by gold today, we have faith when we exchange the $20 bill for goods and services, the person on the other side of the transaction has the same faith in the $20 bill to receive it for goods and services. Bitcoin shares attributes of fiat currency, but is "backed" differently.

What are the characteristics of money?

Durability is one characteristic of money. Money must be durable and cannot get stale or perish. In ancient Rome, soldiers were given salt as payment for service. When it rained, their salt melted away. So salt was valuable, but not durable enough to survive as money. Bitcoin possesses durability, even though it is digital in nature. Bitcoins can exist if a digital wallet is lost or damaged by utilizing a backup to rebuild the digital wallet.

The paper currency we all use is scarce and therefore meets another characteristic of money. There is a finite supply of paper money, right? Bitcoin is also scarce. There will only be 21 million mined[10], thanks to limits established by its creator, who we will discuss shortly.

The next characteristic of money is divisibility. Paper currency can be exchanged easily for different values and reduced to coins or larger and smaller paper currencies. Divisibility is also extremely easy for Bitcoin, in that it is divisible up to eight decimal places.

The final characteristic of money is recognizability. Paper currency is easy to recognize. A person does not have to spend time weighing and testing money and requires little skills to understand it

[10] Why 21 million? That decision was made by Bitcoin's creator, Satoshi Nakamoto.

is a medium of exchange. Bitcoin is easily recognizable for those who understand Bitcoin. Using Bitcoin requires no skill other than understanding the basics of sending and receiving Bitcoin, which is very similar to sending and receiving an email.

Is Bitcoin really money?

One of the arguments that Bitcoin is not money is that it has a market price that floats up and down in value and is quite volatile. Price stability is important in any monetary system, as people need to have confidence their money will be worth something when they need to use it. They also need to know it will have little depreciation in value.

Bitcoin's exchange value volatility makes it problematic if one is looking for complete price stability. But as Bitcoin continues along its growth path, stability will be achieved. We are already seeing Bitcoin becoming more stable.[11]

Economists use a few other measures to help determine whether money is money, but Bitcoin does possess the most important characteristics of money.

---

[11] Inflation presents an interesting conundrum and is found in most monetary systems. Inflation is a measure of how goods and services cost more over time when compared to the past. On the surface, a nation's currency might appear stable. But when indexed to the cost of goods and services, most nations' currency systems are most definitely impacted by rising prices of goods and services. It makes the argument of Bitcoin price stability less an issue in that Bitcoin has no upside limit on what its value might be someday, given that it is scarce.

Bitcoin is backed by math

"In short, Bitcoin is backed by mathematics," according to Bitcoin.org. "With these attributes, all that is required for a form of money to hold value is trust and adoption. In the case of Bitcoin, this can be measured by its growing base of participants. As with all currency, Bitcoin's value comes only and directly from people willing to accept them as payment."

At its most basic level, supply and demand drives the Bitcoin market. Demand for Bitcoin is increasing while the supply is growing at a controlled rate, which it does in the Bitcoin protocol, no matter how many computers are mining simultaneously.[12]

Bitcoin supply is controlled through a rather ingenious throttling mechanism called difficulty. Difficulty is a measure of how difficult it is to find a number below a given target. This number is called a hash.

A hash is a number generated from a string of text. The Bitcoin hash algorithm is used to generate a large and verifiable random number that requires a predictable amount of computing effort to solve. The importance of hashing is that it is used to constrain or ease Bitcoin creation and is used as a supply-side constraint. The larger the hash, the more time it takes to solve the computing problem.

Once solved, the Bitcoin network rewards the miner who solved the block or the hash. The difficulty adjusts every 2016 blocks, which works out to be every 14 days for Bitcoin.[13]

---

[12] Bitcoin possesses a deflationary bias. Because of the limited number of coins to be mined is known (21 million) and the controlled rate the coins are mined, by its nature Bitcoin is deflationary.

How is Bitcoin value derived?

In markets that are free of regulation and intrusion, prices of goods and services are determined by market forces. In free markets, price stability is eventually achieved as market forces reach equilibrium.

Bitcoin price is market-driven, and its price moves up and down on a day-to-day basis, just as other currencies float up and down when pegged to another currency.

Bitcoin price is driven by numerous other factors such as news, governmental actions, taxation, actions and motivations of buyers and sellers in the free market, and psychological factors such as fear and greed. Sounds like the stock market, doesn't it? Bitcoin's price is dependent on market forces.

These are the basics you'll need to know and understand as we move into the more detailed and analytical chapters to follow.

---

[13] Each cryptocurrency has its own metrics. They are the hashing algorithm used, total number of coins to be mined, network difficulty level retargeting, halving rate and number of coins awarded per block.

3 The History of Bitcoin

Bitcoin was first discussed in 1998, about the time the Internet itself was gaining traction. It was started by members of the Cypherpunks mailing list, which was one of the first online mailing lists of its kind. Members could send and receive email to a particular address, and conversations could be carried on concerning various topics. For the first time, it allowed people from all over the world to communicate on various topics that interested them. One of those topics was the concept of online currencies.

Wei Dai is given credit for starting the Cypherpunks discussion on the concept of cryptocurrency. His idea was to create a new currency that uses cryptography and a network of interconnected computers to control the creation of the currency and manage the transactions, rather than having a single authority like a central government or an entity like the United States Federal Reserve. Wei's idea was to eliminate all the middlemen who influence, manipulate or control monetary systems.

Examples of middlemen are governments, reserve banks, commercial banks, brokerages and merchant networks. All have subtle to profound influences on monetary systems and ultimately their populace, both in how they are designed and controlled and also their efficiencies. Whether you view it as merely evolutionary or revolutionary, Bitcoin can trace its roots back to Wei.

Now fast-forward 10 years to 2008. The Cypherpunks mailing list members were still communicating back and forth about various topics. One was a member we believe to be from Japan named Satoshi Nakamoto. We say "we believe" because his true identity has never been confirmed, as he has chosen to remain anonymous.

At   http://p2pfoundation.ning.com/profile/SatoshiNakamoto, Nakamoto published a profile in which he claimed to be a 37-year-old man living in Japan. That was met with skepticism due to his use of English and his Bitcoin software code not being documented nor commented in Japanese.

In 2008, Nakamoto published a paper in which he proposed processes and methods to implement a currency system which we now call Bitcoin. His primary goal was to introduce a system for electronic transactions in which trust was not a factor in the transaction.

The first Bitcoins were pre-mined by Nakamoto in January 2009. The first block of Bitcoins, called the "genesis block," started with 50 Bitcoins. Nakamoto was part of the project until late 2010, after which he seemed to vanish from most of the places he frequented online. He did not reveal much about himself. No one knows for sure where Nakamoto lives. We do not know if he is a real person.

There have been a couple of high-profile stories in recent years which claimed to reveal the true identity of Nakamoto. In one case, Newsweek magazine claimed to have tracked him down in California, but the man they named vehemently denied the story. In 2016, Australian businessman Craig Wright came forward claiming to be Nakamoto. There were both believers and doubters, but there is not yet a consensus belief that Wright is who he claims to be.

There is speculation Nakamoto is actually a collection of people who worked together on this complex project. That would explain why no one person stepped forward to take credit for it in the press or speak about it publicly, until Wright.

There's a lot of mystery around Bitcoin, and some people have tried to turn that into a negative – speculating perhaps this person or group benefited financially in a large way as being an integral part of the creation of Bitcoin where he or they "pre-mined" Bitcoins ahead of Bitcoin's initial release. There is no proof of that. But there is little doubt Nakamoto proposed a system that had the potential to create a paradigm shift in the financial world. We are seeing such a shift today.

The paper is still available, and you can download it here, http://Bitcoin.org/Bitcoin.pdf. You can review his theories, his concepts and mathematical formulas that created Bitcoin.

Perhaps someday it will be revealed who Nakamoto really is. Right now, he holds mythical status, and for now, his true identity remains a mystery. It is the stuff of which legends are made.

4 Why Bitcoin is Important

You might be asking, why create Bitcoin? Does the world really need a new type of currency? Both are very good questions that need answers.

In the beginning, Bitcoin started out as discussion and then an experiment. It appealed to freethinkers, libertarians and, to a degree, people who had an axe to grind with entities that control monetary systems, like the Federal Reserve in the U.S.

Many new ideas start out as revolutionary but then are accepted as evolutionary. As the ideas are understood and explored, they are either adopted or rejected as being unworthy of pursuit. This is exactly what has happened with Bitcoin. Acceptance and adoption is occurring at a blindingly fast pace. It was a great idea, and we are seeing its implementation integrating more and more into the mainstream with each passing day.

One key to answering the question of why the Cypherpunks community felt the need to create a digital currency is the concept of trust. Trust is needed when we transact business with any currency. But is trust needed on a payment network? Or better yet, does trust create problems with a payment network?

Drawbacks with Traditional Payment Networks

To make traditional payment networks secure, all network participants must be vetted to make sure allowing access on the network won't be harmful to the network and its users. Most payment networks are centralized and only a small percentage of people can be trusted enough not to commit malicious or fraudulent acts on the network. In this model, the assumption is that people cannot be trusted.

Traditional credit card merchant networks are an example of this type of trust model, and it's very common to hear about some security breach that injures the payment network, costs the merchant networks billions of dollars a year in losses and expenses because of breaches and the security costs needed to protect the network. These costs are ultimately passed on to the consumers in price increases in the cost of goods and services they purchase.

Trust can only stretch so far in a digital world, given the pace and sheer volume of transactions that need to be monitored and approved. Also in an ever-increasingly interconnected world, traditional payment networks are subject to breaches and hacking. There has to be a better payment network; a network that is not built upon trust. There is and it is Bitcoin.

There Has to Be a Better Payment Network

The community behind Bitcoin attempted to create, in basic terms, money for the Internet using a payment system where trust was not a factor in its operation. The community felt there was a need for a completely digital money because of the aforementioned problems found in most payment systems. Most traditional payment systems don't work well for Internet transactions.

The designer(s) of Bitcoin wanted money specific for the Internet that has no single central authority controlling it. Also, a major objective was a money system powered by the users where trust isn't a factor in securing and maintaining the integrity of the network. You might want to ponder the last sentence for a few minutes and let the power of the idea sink into your mind, as it the primary reason for Bitcoin's existence.

Bitcoin and the protocols governing Bitcoin create a very secure payment system. Transactions are encrypted at the point of origin and sent across the payment network where trust isn't needed for those participating on the network.

The payment network doesn't care whether you are a good person or bad person, criminal, communist, anarchist or capitalist. The payment network is secured by mathematics and encryption, and its role is to confirm transactions and add them to the blockchain. The assumption is no one can be trusted, so the community built a network where all can participate in moving Bitcoin around the planet while avoiding all the problems that a closed-loop payment system possesses.

Does Bitcoin solve all the problems inherent with money? No it doesn't. The points of failure are mostly with online exchanges, which are attached to the core Bitcoin framework by their respective creators. Bitcoin's core functionality does not include conversion into fiat currencies, which is why the exchanges (and their non-Bitcoin technology) have emerged. The only way for most people to comprehend Bitcoin's value is by comparing its value to their own fiat currency.

These exchanges often don't use best practices to secure client funds, and their internal networks are often vulnerable, leaving them open to hacking and theft. Most money lost with Bitcoin has come from Bitcoin exchanges not doing the right things to protect their internal networks and their customers' Bitcoins. It is important to understand there isn't a problem with Bitcoin or the protocols governing it as those are solid and reliable and protected by encryption and mathematics. The problem is with the outside entities trying to integrate with the system and not having systems as secure as the core Bitcoin protocol.

Anonymity

Anonymity is another reason Bitcoin was created. Anonymity is the ability to exchange Bitcoin without the name and other identifiable contact information of the person making or receiving the transaction being known publicly. There are positive reasons to remain anonymous, and there are also reasons many would view as negative.

For the currency we carry in our physical wallets, the transactions between individuals are mostly anonymous to the rest of the world. No one knows about them unless they actually see the transaction occur between individuals or businesses. Those transactions can be positive, or they can be negative in their impact to an individual or to society.

A positive transaction could be spending cash to buy present a gift for a loved one for his or her birthday. A negative transaction could be spending cash in an illegal drug deal.

So even with fiat currency that we hold in our hands every day, there can be ethical or moral issues, just as there are with cryptocurrencies. It depends upon who is holding the money and what it is being used for. Bitcoin is not much different than cash in that it can be used for good and bad in a mostly anonymous manner.

No Central Authority

No one person or entity actually controls Bitcoin. This is another reason for the creation of Bitcoin. As mentioned in the "What is Bitcoin" chapter, the payment network is completely decentralized. Computers on the Internet running software are what move the payments from peer to peer, or account to account.

People and entities who seem have problems grasping Bitcoin view the lack of authority as some deviant, unethical or sinister plot that must be exposed. Oftentimes, confusion creates misunderstandings about what no central authority actually means.

It's not some spooky plot unfolding to destabilize or undermine government's control of money. It is about decentralizing how transactions are processed. Decentralization is actually a good thing.

We value it for hours every day that we spend time on the Internet, the most decentralized network in existence. It provides the framework and context for much of our daily lives now. It was scary for some in its beginning, but now it is firmly rooted into most of our lives. We now take the Internet for granted, and it's part of our daily lives.

Understand there are hundreds of millions of computers, smartphones, tablets, smart televisions and other devices that are all connected to the Internet with no central authority -- and it works flawlessly most of the time. It's simply amazing to think about how we can bounce information from one part of the world to another without any care or concern on how it gets there -- it just does!

There are standards and protocols that govern the movement of information around the Internet. The protocols assure the integrity of the network, meaning we can have a high degree of confidence that information will get to where it is supposed go.   It's all controlled by the protocols.

Because the Internet is decentralized, it can continue moving information intelligently even if a part of the Internet is having issues. The Internet knows how to reroute information in the event of parts of the Internet going down or offline through robust and intelligent routing mechanisms.

Bitcoin rides over the Internet protocols just like video and voice. Because Bitcoin transactions are encrypted at point of origin, a sender's transaction moves safely and swiftly from peer to peer (computer to computer), finding its way to the right recipient. If one computer along the way goes offline, another peer will step up and continue to route the transaction until finding the intended recipient.

So don't let fear grip you any longer when you hear the words "no central authority." It's really the technology that is misunderstood and being demonized -- not some anti-government plot at work. Bitcoin and its protocols are simply providing a new type of payment platform that works well for Internet transactions. The reader should look at the motives behind those who find fault with Bitcoin and see if they have an alternative agenda. In most cases, they have something to lose if Bitcoin succeeds.

In the next chapter, we examine the pros and cons of a decentralized money supply.

5 The Importance of Decentralization

A critical feature of Bitcoin or any cryptocurrency is decentralization. We mentioned previously Bitcoin is an option to state-issued currency, also known as fiat currency.

Because of Bitcoin's very nature, the way it is created, and the way its transactions are generated, transactions move in an unregulated fashion. The transactions move "peer to peer," or computer to computer. Bitcoin works on a network where users get together to cut out the middlemen, which usually are the banks, merchant networks and, yes, even governments.

When people transfer Bitcoin peer to peer (i.e. individual to individual, individual to business or business to business), there is not an intermediary, such as a bank or credit card company. The network helps to ensure the transactions are valid. Unlike credit card fraud, with Bitcoin you cannot easily commit fraud by spending money you do not have -- known as a "double spend." The transactions are validated almost instantaneously through a process called confirmation, as described in the previous chapter.

Confidence in Bitcoin is gained when one understands how transactions occur, how you move money from your "wallet" to someone else's "wallet" or to a business, and how transactions are confirmed. A Bitcoin transaction goes through a confirmation process in which it is validated numerous times in the mining process.

Statistically speaking, you can count on a Bitcoin transaction being valid within six confirmations. Once you have six confirmations, you can count on the transaction being fully confirmed, avoiding the double-spend risk. This takes a little bit of time to occur because there are computers on the network where confirmation activity is taking place. It is decentralized – peer to peer – and not in a central database or server.

One of the drawbacks of Bitcoin is that it can take up to 45 minutes to an hour for a transaction to be statistically confirmed six times. So if you're dealing with commerce, the time it takes for full confirmation would be a drawback.

This confirmation delay led to a group of individuals and companies that are among the leaders in Bitcoin mining to create a new version of Bitcoin in August 2017 known as Bitcoin Cash. This new version has more memory capacity in its blockchain, so transactions can be confirmed more quickly by supercomputers assigned to the task. The creators of Bitcoin Cash believe their offshoot of Bitcoin will become the primary means of cryptocurrency payment because it will be more efficient to use at a point of sale. After all, would you wait 45 minutes at a retailer's cash register to complete your purchase? (It's not clear at the time this book was written just how much quicker Bitcoin Cash transactions are confirmed than the legacy Bitcoin.)

As a result of the lengthy confirmation process, merchants who accept Bitcoin have the option of reducing the number of confirmations necessary for a transaction to be considered official and for the merchant to have access to the Bitcoin received. For merchants who deal in very small increments (also known as "MilliBits" or mBTC which will be discussed later), fewer confirmations may be an acceptable risk because the amount being sent to their wallets is relatively small.

Bitcoin exchanges, which process transactions involving much higher amounts typically, usually go with the full six confirmations. It's a security measure which doesn't interfere with the purchase process. Most people buying or selling Bitcoins understand it's a higher-level transaction than buying coffee at a coffee shop. While you're not going to wait an hour for your coffee, you will certainly be tolerant for a transaction of higher amounts to be fully confirmed for the comfort of both the buyer and seller.

In a retail environment where transactions need to take place quickly, the delay for full confirmation can be problematic. But the founders or visionaries behind the Bitcoin were actually looking into the future.

For example, right now you can, with smartphones, install wallets with which you can transact business very quickly. The confirmations happen quickly, with an hour being the maximum amount of time it can take to confirm. After you get three confirmations, you can be quite confident in the validity of the Bitcoin sent to you, even though it is not at the threshold of the statistically significant six confirmations. The authors of this book have not personally witnessed a double-spend issue, but it is a possibility, which is why we recommend waiting on six confirmations to be sure the transaction is valid if the transaction size warrants such a wait.

How Bitcoin will affect the world's existing fiat currencies

The world's governments are grappling with how they should or can regulate the cryptocurrencies to help protect consumers and assure compliance with laws and taxation. But at this point in time, regulation is limited to the transactions when you exchange Bitcoin to your local currency. Unless Bitcoin has been either outlawed by a government or fully accepted as legal tender by a government, there is not much control or regulatory power that government has in either case.

There are Bitcoin exchanges in the United States, as well as all over the world, including Coinbase, which we referenced earlier. We use and recommend it, and it is very easy to set up an account there. They do not ask for a lot of personal information.

You can link your bank account a Coinbase account, convert a Bitcoin to U.S. dollars in minutes, and have money in your bank account in U.S. dollars within two or three business days.

Because Coinbase is widely considered the most robust Bitcoin exchange in the U.S., the IRS decided in early 2017 to see if it could find a way to collect some taxes from the growing number of Bitcoin investors and traders. Originally seeking information from Coinbase on all its customers who bought or sold Bitcoin between 2013 and 2015, the IRS relented, and instead is focusing its efforts on transactions involving $20,000 USD or more. Coinbase users were still fighting the IRS action as of the publication of this book.

This case illustrates that not only are governments going to come calling sooner or later, but also that Coinbase is fighting the IRS -- something its customers certainly appreciate.

Governmental tracking removes one of the elements people find attractive about cryptocurrencies – that the transactions occur peer to peer, individual to individual or business to business, directly between the two, with no intermediary. But as long as you are using software wallets local on your computer and conduct transactions only in cryptocurrencies (without conversion to a fiat currency), then transparency can still be achieved.

At this point in time, it's only when you want to convert back to the local currency where you live that the governments might be interested in knowing what is going on.

The Canadian government is one of the first to create its own cryptocurrency, known as the MintChip.

A MintChip is a secure smart card chip, which may be integrated with a secure digital (SD) card for easier connection to computers and mobile devices. The card contains a private key signed by the Canadian mint, which is itself then used to sign transactions. When making a payment, the sender gets the ID of the receiver. The chip debits the balance stored within it, and signs a message stating it has done so and the recipient's ID should increment its balance accordingly. This message is then presented to the recipient's chip, which verifies the signatures and adjusts its own balance. Its use is still experimental and limited.

We look for other governments to follow, as they try to emulate some of the benefits of having a cryptocurrency.

The state of New York issued informational subpoenas in late 2013 to various Bitcoin companies operating in the U.S., summoning them to testify in front of committees.

The Wall Street Journal reported around two dozen Bitcoin companies were issued with subpoenas. Coinsetter company founder Jaron Lukasiewicz told coindesk.com he believes the move created the opportunity for Bitcoin companies to work with regulators to create an environment in which virtual currency can thrive.

"The companies you most often hear about in the Bitcoin space take regulation very seriously, and are working hard to do things the right way. I view this new dialogue as an opportunity to do that," he told the website.

As far as we know, no one has gotten in trouble or has done anything illegal by simply possessing Bitcoin. But as with all forms of money, what you spend your money on can get you in trouble.

That was the case for the so-called Silk Road, a largely unknown and dark sector of the Internet where illegal drugs were bought and sold, and other questionable business practices were conducted. Bitcoin was the currency, or the method of payment, for Silk Road.

At one point, 30 percent of the daily volume of Bitcoin trading was attributed to the Silk Road, which was shut down in October 2013. The gentleman who started it was arrested and, just before Christmas 2013, Ross Ulbricht of San Francisco asked federal officials to return 144,336 Bitcoins they seized from his computer. With their value around $1,000 apiece at the time, you can understand why he would want them back. He said in a legal filing the currency should be returned because it wasn't subject to civil forfeiture rules. (Can't knock a guy for trying.)

Instead, the U.S. government auctioned off nearly 30,000 of the seized Silk Road Bitcoins in late June 2014, and the auction was won by venture capitalist Tim Draper. At their approximate value at the time of around $600 per Bitcoin, Draper came into possession of nearly $18 million worth of Bitcoins. (The purchase price was not disclosed.)

Reportedly, the government will not sell off the remaining 114,000 or so Bitcoins it seized from Ulbricht unless forced to do so by court order. If Bitcoin values ever grow to the tens of thousands of dollars some experts predict, maybe someday you'll see the government sell off Bitcoins to retire federal debt. At the time of this writing, the Bitcoins being held by the U.S. government were worth a total of $456 million.

Federal prosecutors in New York say Ulbricht went by the online handle the Dread Pirate Roberts and turned the underground site into a place where anonymous users could buy or sell contraband and illegal services.

When Silk Road was shut down, it severely impacted the Bitcoin price and created a short-term panic and subsequent sell-off. It could've been that a lot of people using Bitcoin for nefarious activities needed to liquidate quickly. Or, it could have been due to the market trying to understand what had happened (i.e., digesting the news). At that time, Bitcoin was trading at around $200.

It suffered a setback for a few weeks. Then it started to appreciate and gain value out of that downward movement. It went as high as the $1,200 USD range in late 2013 before settling in around the $700 to $800 USD range around the end of the year.

In case it is not clear by this point, there is nothing nefarious or illegal about participating in Bitcoin trade. Any illegality comes only with what you buy with the coin. If you are buying or selling illegal drugs or items, then you could be in as much trouble with authorities as if you are using cash. The use of Bitcoin in and of itself is not a crime.

Why do people trust Bitcoin?

This might sound like an oxymoron, but most of the trust in Bitcoin is due to the fact that it requires no trust. Because it is a fully open source and decentralized currency, anyone has access to the entire source code at any time. While that doesn't mean much to the average user, it means everything to the computer geeks who are at the heart of developing and maintaining the system.

Developers and interested parties all around the world can verify exactly how Bitcoin works. The same is true for all of the other cryptocurrencies that use the same basic source code as Bitcoin, which is the vast majority of them. Why do they all use the same open-source coding? Because it's working.

It's also important that all the transactions and Bitcoin in existence can be transparently consulted in real time by everyone. There is a record, the blockchain. Even though Bitcoin ownership is anonymous, we know how many Bitcoin there are in existence at any one moment. We know exactly how many there are -- unlike governments, which have to publish their monetary statistics only on a quarterly basis and are subject to frequent revisions and restatements.

All Bitcoin transactions in history are available for review, if we wish. They are transparent. But at the same time, we do not know who the parties to the transaction were. All payments can be made in confidence because a third party (the anonymous "miner") is running or executing the cryptographic algorithms. Much of the technology that banks use to protect transactions is being used with Bitcoin.

Finally, as we have mentioned previously, no organization or individual can control Bitcoin. The network is secure, even if not all the uses and users can be trusted. It means there might be some people out there trying to figure out ways to injure the Bitcoin network, but those actions do not impact the payment system. There may be people out there doing things wrong, but it still remains secure as a whole.

Later in this book, we talk about the risks related to Bitcoin, and what you can do to mitigate risk or control the risk. You can't eliminate all risk in life, but there are some things we can do with Bitcoin to make them more secure.

6 Bitcoin Mining: The Gold Rush

Mining Bitcoins is one of the primary ways to acquire Bitcoins. There are a few similarities between the gold rush of the 1800s in California and Alaska and the current rush to mine or otherwise acquire Bitcoins in the 21st century. The primary connection between the two is an opportunity for the masses is to mine something of value.

When you are "mining" Bitcoins, you don't use an actual pick or shovel. The term "mining" is analogous to mining for gold or other precious metals. In physical mining, a worker digs for the precious metal. Bitcoin has adopted that same nomenclature for the online creation of that currency.

No one performs physical work to mine Bitcoins. Instead, computers are whirring around the globe to solve complex encryption problems (a process known as "hashing") while packaging up Bitcoin transactions. When one encryption task is solved, the person whose computer solved the task is rewarded with Bitcoins.

In the early days of Bitcoin, around 2009, a regular home computer with a normal CPU (computer processing unit) could mine coins easily. It was possible to accumulate them with a home computer. Now, as time has elapsed and more coins were created, it has become more difficult to create coins, and that is how Satoshi Nakamoto intended for the system to develop and mature.

This is analogous to the gold rush days in California and Alaska in the 1800s. It was relatively easy to find gold when people first began to hunt for it. As more and more was mined, it became increasingly difficult. Now, it requires sophisticated mining operations to mine successfully for gold anywhere in the world.

There are similarities to mining Bitcoin, which has turned into its own industry. There are supercomputer farms around the globe, and their only purpose is to utilize nearly unimaginable "hashing" power to solve the equations needed to earn new Bitcoin. These supercomputer operations are all racing each other, effectively eliminating personal computers as a way to mine Bitcoin. There's no way your PC is going to have more processing power than scores and scores of supercomputers.

To gain a better understanding of Bitcoin mining, we need to go back to how Bitcoins were mined initially, and move forward to today.

Types of mining hardware

There are four types of mining hardware, also known as mining rigs. First, there are the CPUs (central processing units, usually traditional computers like your desktop computer). Few mine with CPUs anymore. You have as much chance of your home computer beating a high-powered computer "rig" to solve a computation and earn Bitcoin as you do of finding a needle in a haystack.

There are also GPUs (graphics processing units), which are mainly the high-end gaming computers that have expensive graphics boards. The complex problems that need to be solved can be offloaded to the graphics board. The graphics board can perform the encryption or hashing calculations much faster than a CPU. GPUs are normally used to mine other cryptocurrencies, not Bitcoin.

The next step in the mining technology progression is the field-programmable gate array (FPGA). It is a semiconductor device that can be programmed after manufacturing. Just think of it as a chip that can be programmed. FPGAs are faster than CPUs and GPUs, but slower than our next type of mining hardware.

Mining Bitcoin today for the most part uses technology called an application specific computer chip (ASIC), which is specialized hardware that only does one thing: It mines cryptocurrencies. It does not do anything else.

With ASIC machines, you are not restricted to mining Bitcoins. You can mine many of the other cryptocurrencies that support the mining algorithm for that ASIC device.

Deeper dive into mining hardware

ASIC hardware is very expensive. It starts out in the multiple thousands for a good ASIC unit. The benefit is they mine incredibly fast. We used to talk about computer processor speeds in terms of megahertz. Then we talked in terms of gigahertz. Now we still talk about the speed, but in terms of how profitable the processes are. In measuring performance of digital money, it is called a hash.

The hash rate is the speed at which a computer completes an operation in the Bitcoin code. A higher hashrate is better when mining, as it increases your opportunity of finding the next block and receiving the reward before another miner does.

In January of 2013, the "hash rate" at which Bitcoin problems were being solved system-wide was about 20,000 gigaHash per second. Move to August 2017, and the rate had jumped to 7 million teraHash (trillions of hashes) per second.

What is fueling the continued growth? It's the number of individuals and companies who activated Bitcoin mining hardware. They're all being driven by the hope to accumulate Bitcoins in an appreciating market, motivated to make a profit.

The goal of a Bitcoin (or other cryptocurrency) mining operation is to maximize your hashing rate with your Bitcoin hardware to the extent that will allow you to:

a) mine more coins than it will cost you in electricity to operate the equipment; and
b) make as large of a profit as you can.

The higher your Hash rate, the greater your chance to mine coins of value. ASICS are specific to cryptocurrency mining. When they aren't mining, they are big paperweights, or they make great bookends.

We don't recommend you mine Bitcoin with GPU. It will cost you more in electricity to run the computer than the amount of Bitcoin your GPU will generate.

Mining methods

As this book is being written, there are two primary mining methods or algorithms in computing parlance. They are scrypt mining and SHA256 mining. There are spinoffs or derivations to these algorithms. There are groups also tinkering with other mining algorithms.

We're not going to get too deep into the highly technical differences between the two primary methods. But it's good to understand that the SHA256 mining is used primarily with Bitcoin, and scrypt mining is used with alternative cryptocurrencies such as Litecoin and others.

There are possible advantages to mining the newer cryptocurrencies instead of Bitcoin. Because the other cryptocurrencies are newer, the difficulty level is substantially lower. One is able to mine a lot of coins at a very low price, or accumulate a large number of coins very quickly in the hope that one of those coins will become established as a player in the cryptocurrency community.

Other ways to mine

The other way to participate in mining is called "cloud hashing." Companies are setting up data centers with immense ASIC processing power available for purchase at an affordable rate. You buy a contract or multiple contracts for part of the processing power of their hashing network for a period of time, usually a year. There are websites where you can buy and sell hashing power. You can spend as little as a couple hundred dollars and buy a decent amount of processing power. You can also spend tens of thousands of dollars on a business-level contract. We've even heard of contract purchases in the million-dollar range.

The more you are willing to invest in contracts, the greater return in Bitcoin you receive. You literally are able to buy in at a low rate and fix your basis. So as the Bitcoin appreciates in value, your return on investment can be phenomenal if Bitcoin continues to appreciate in value.

Proceed with caution

We strongly advise you to exercise caution and due diligence when investing at this point in either mining equipment or cloud hashing. As mentioned earlier, there are supercomputer farms around the globe that have essentially taken over Bitcoin mining. If you have anything less than a supercomputer, your chance of losing money by spending more on the electricity to run the mining computer than the value of coins you mine is quite high.

There are still opportunities for new millionaires to be created by mining some of the alternative cryptocurrencies, which we will address later in the book. You have to be lucky and choose one that becomes a major player. Whether one of the newer ones can actually achieve more value than Bitcoin is yet to be seen.

The market is volatile, and by the time you are reading this book, changes are very likely.

7 Three Kinds of Wallets

There are three primary kinds of Bitcoin and cryptocurrency wallets[14]:

- Desktop wallet
- Mobile wallet
- Web wallet

No matter what cryptocurrency you use, you are always going to need a software wallet.

A **desktop wallet** is software on your computer, so it is local. It gives you more control over your wallet, which at the same time makes you responsible for protecting the money in your wallet and also doing backups. You are, in effect, ultimately responsible -- you ARE the bank. There are several desktop wallets available for Bitcoin. Visit Bitcoin.org's directory of available software wallets at https://bitcoin.org/en/choose-your-wallet.

---

[14] There are other types of Bitcoin wallets, like a Brain Wallet. We chose to focus solely on the most common wallets.

Mobile wallets are applications you install on your mobile phone. You physically store your coins in the mobile wallet and you are able to pay stores and businesses or individuals by scanning a QR code. For example, if you are paying a store, the store would generate a QR code with their receiver address. Then you scan that with your wallet and type in the amount of money you want to send them in Bitcoin or whatever currency you want to send to them. Then you would transmit it.

The sending and receiving addresses are both quite long, full of seemingly random characters. Because of that, it's really hard to just tell somebody what the wallet address is. So QR codes are used. Today we are even using near field communication technology, in which you tap to pay. Visit Bitcoin.org's directory of available mobile wallets at https://bitcoin.org/en/choose-your-wallet. With some of the newer cryptocurrencies out today, you may not always be able to find a mobile wallet or a web wallet.

A **web wallet** takes the least amount of effort to get set up. It allows you to store Bitcoin or other cryptocurrency anywhere you can access the web. There is less effort needed to protect a web wallet, but you really have to be super careful who you allow to host the wallet. There have been a few cases where wallets were hacked. If you have your coins stored in a web wallet that gets hacked, they are gone. There is no recourse. Some of these companies exist and then disappear. You want to practice due diligence if you are going to use web wallets. Visit Bitcoin.org's directory of available web wallets at https://bitcoin.org/en/choose-your-wallet.

Our recommended web wallet is Coinbase. We highly recommend that you research whatever company you are entrusting your coins with to make sure they are reputable and they seem to be taking the necessary security cautions with your coins.

Among Coinbase's excellent security measures are that they do paper backups of wallets and keep them off-site, too. These are encrypted, meaning even they cannot decrypt them, because they do not have the key (which is a function of the individual password for each wallet). They do not know it. So if someone were to do some sort of man-in-the-middle attack or find a piece of paper or steal the flash drive, the wallet can only be decrypted by the individual keying in the password.

Bitcoin is an open-source project. That means the codes for creating wallets themselves are open source, available for inspection by anybody who wants to look at them. At the same time, there is a license that allows other cryptocurrencies to actually use the original source code used to create the original Bitcoin wallet.

Desktop wallets for your computer

The original Bitcoin software wallet is called Bitcoin QT. You have other cryptocurrencies using the same software. Bitcoin QT is a full Bitcoin client available for Windows, Linux and Mac. You can download it directly from Bitcoin.org and have it up and running fairly quickly.

Another software wallet a lot of people use which is also available for Mac, Linux and Windows is called MultiBit. A real lightweight client, it is fast and it is easy to use. It is also synchronized with the network quickly.

Whenever you install a new wallet, it has to go out to the Internet and download the blockchain since the beginning of time for that particular cryptocurrency. It includes every transaction that has occurred. So literally, it can take hours or days depending on

Internet speed to get your wallet set up if you are using something like Bitcoin QT. MultiBit clients synchronize quicker.

The third of the "big three" desktop wallets is Armory for Windows and Linux. It is a really advanced client that extends features and functionality. It's mainly used by power users. It offers encryption and secure cold storage of wallets. That means you can move your wallet onto a piece of paper that's obviously not connected to the Internet – another way to protect and preserve your wallet.

People who have large amounts of Bitcoin should use Armory and keep most of their coins in cold storage. The obvious advantage to being on a computer not hooked to the Internet is you cannot get easily hacked.

Mobile wallets for your phone and tablet

Many different mobile wallets have been developed. There is a Bitcoin wallet available in the Google play android app store by doing a search for Bitcoin wallet. It is a good choice for non-technical people, and it is also available for Blackberry.

Several Bitcoin apps in the Apple app store are so new we have not been able to evaluate them yet. Coinbase was one of several companies that had their mobile Bitcoin wallet apps removed from the Apple app store in early 2014 -- around the time Bitcoin value was dwindling and the world's top Bitcoin exchange in terms of volume, Japan-based Mt. Gox, collapsed and left customers unable to access 750,000 of their Bitcoins they had stored there.

Apple at that time took down all Bitcoin-related apps in a precautionary move. Like many other individuals and companies at the time, Apple wanted to evaluate the reliability of the Bitcoin infrastructure to ensure users of Bitcoin-related apps downloaded from Apple weren't exposing themselves to possible fraud or theft. After some due diligence and some very strong reaction from the Bitcoin community, Apple slowly began reintroducing Bitcoin-related mobile apps, including the Coinbase app, in mid-2014.

Web wallets: Store your coins in the cloud

There are quite a few web wallet companies. Blockchain.info has been very popular, along with Coinbase.

The thing about a web wallet is that anywhere you have secure web access, you can use it – emphasis on SECURE web access.

You should never access a web wallet at an Internet café. If you are on your personal laptop in an Internet cafe and you have a secure connection to your wallet, all use SSL security, so it would be safe to access your wallet there.

The cool thing about web wallets is you can move money around wherever you are if there is an Internet connection available. You do not have to have physical access to your smartphone or to your computer. Also the theft risk is reduced -- for example, if someone were to steal your mobile phone or your computer, or if your hard drive were to crash.

One of features of web wallets like Coinbase is if we convert Bitcoin to fiat currency, they would actually transfer it to our bank account within two business days. We get the market price at the moment that we sell the Bitcoin.

Let's say Bitcoin is trading at $4,300 USD, and we decide we want to sell one Bitcoin at Coinbase. And, let's say while they give us the money over the next two days, Bitcoin values go down significantly, maybe in the $3,600 range. Well, we still get the $4,300 because we locked in our price at the moment when we exchanged our coins for dollars. That is a nice feature.

Trading exchanges -- places where you can convert one cryptocurrency to another cryptocurrency -- are being developed at a rapid pace. It may be that you convert one cryptocurrency to the U.S. dollar, the British pound, the Japanese yen, or whatever the currency may be. You can literally hold all sorts of currencies.

8 Bitcoin for Business

If you are a business owner, there are specific companies that have developed Bitcoin shopping carts that can be integrated into your existing payment processing system. Just as there are Visa, MasterCard, and American Express payment platforms, there are Bitcoin payment platforms.

When a person drops something in the online shopping cart and goes to the checkout process, the transaction is in the local currency most of the time. But with the new Bitcoin shopping cart functionality, as they work their way through the checkout process, they literally are choosing whether they want to pay with a credit card or pay with Bitcoin.

If they choose to pay with Bitcoin, the cart interfaces with the payment platform and figures out what the market price is at that particular moment. It locks in the price for a period of time for the transaction to complete.

The premier payment platform at the time this book is being written is BitPay. They have different pricing levels. The starting level is a 1 percent transaction fee. They support over 20 different online shopping carts, with WordPress being one of them.

They do daily bank deposits to your account, which is different from merchant accounts. People have to the wait two to three days for money to clear with merchant accounts. You don't have to do that because there are no fraud concerns here. There's no worry about chargebacks because Bitcoin transactions are final. Once you send Bitcoin to someone or to a business, there is no way you can recall it. There's no way you can ask for it to come back to your wallet. It is done. There are other pricing plans that include priority phone support and the ability to import sales into QuickBooks.

BitPay is a company that seems very aggressive. It is very simple for a programmer to integrate their API (application programming interface).

There is a whole industry being built right now -- building the infrastructure for payment platforms. If you are a business owner and you want to add Bitcoin integration into your website, then it's becoming much easier to do.

Food, electronics, precious metals, in addition to web services and gifts, are the types of companies most often using Bitcoin payment integration. It's a good thing for businesses.

We're at the tipping point right now where if you're in a particular industry that has international clientele, you could get a lot of positive press for accepting Bitcoin in your industry. If you are the first, you may generate a lot of business for yourself by doing so. Many people are hungry to spend the Bitcoin.

One example of a business that struck early was Overstock.com. After announcing in December 2013 they intended to accept Bitcoin at some point in 2014, they exceeded all expectations and launched their Bitcoin acceptance feature in early January. When they did, people with Bitcoin were eager to spend it. In their first day accepting Bitcoin, Overstock.com did more than $120,000 USD worth of business in Bitcoin.

More recently, some of the companies you certainly will recognize that have either begun to accept Bitcoin, or announced they will do so, include Dish Network, Dell Computer, WordPress, and Microsoft. Tiger Direct, a leading online retailer of tech and electronic products, was close behind Overstock.com in announcing its acceptance of Bitcoin. Expedia.com started accepting Bitcoin for hotel reservations only in mid-2014 as they work out kinks in their own system.

Companies this large don't make changes like this unless they have vetted the idea for all possible negative impacts. It is clear that more and more large companies are understanding they will receive both a positive reaction from customers, and a positive public relations boost, from accepting Bitcoin. If you have a needed product or service, then people are going to want to do business with you. There are a lot of opportunities there for merchants.

In order to send and receive Bitcoins, you will have to have a Bitcoin wallet. You can carry it with you, most likely on your smartphone or tablet. It will be loaded with Bitcoins.

Let's say you wanted to sell us a pizza. You would tell us what the pizza cost. It can be in Bitcoins or your local currency. Let's say it is worth $10. What we would do is calculate what fractional share of the Bitcoin we need to send so we can buy the pizza. All this can be done very quickly, within seconds or minutes at the most. When we have your receiver address, we send that Bitcoin there. Within seconds, it shows up in your wallet, the transaction is completed, and you can comfortably give me the pizza.

This is forward thinking, similar to near field communications or low-power Bluetooth being adopted by the credit card companies and smartphone manufacturers.

Near field communication (NFC) is a set of standards for smartphones and similar devices to establish radio communication with each other by touching them together or bringing them into close proximity, usually no more than a few centimeters. According to the respected website Mashable.com, present and anticipated applications include contactless transactions, data exchange, and simplified setup of more complex communications such as Wi-Fi. Communication is also possible between an NFC device and an unpowered NFC chip, called a "tag."

There is nothing that would prevent us from having near field technology with a Bitcoin merchant terminal. You could go into a flower shop, for example, and use your phone to send a fractional share of a Bitcoin to a flower arranger to create a gift for your spouse. It can all be done through near field communication, where there exists the huge advantage of not having to get the sender's or receiver's address. All that would be eliminated by having a terminal where this communication is taking place securely.

We envision a person being able to have multiple Bitcoin or cryptocurrency wallets, just like you have Visa, MasterCard and American Express. Even with those cards, you have differing companies that run the cards. You could have multiple wallets in the same smartphone, with different cryptocurrencies loaded in each of them.

You might use Bitcoin for a big-ticket purchase like buying a big-screen television. You might use, for example, Litecoins for something smaller. You can diversify your holdings, and have different cryptocurrencies on your phone for different purposes.

However, a word of caution: If your phone gets stolen or lost or dropped in a bucket of water or your phone somehow is destroyed, then those coins are lost forever. So we don't recommend keeping currencies local on your phone yet. You should use a reputable cloud-based wallet.

9 Where to Spend Bitcoins

There are numerous places where you can spend your Bitcoins. Remember Bitcoins were created primarily to be used on the Internet. There are places popping up every day online where you can use your coins to buy products and services.

For example, there's one company, gyft.com, which will accept Bitcoins and convert them into gift cards. Within minutes, you can convert your Bitcoin into gift cards of various denominations. The same company also has Amazon.com gift cards available. There are hundreds of choices. You can do a search on that site, and if you're seeking a card from a well-known brand, chances are good it will be available there.

There are also places where you can walk in the door and they will accept Bitcoin. Those brick and mortar locations will display a Bitcoin logo, similar to the Visa or MasterCard decals you see in the windows of shops that accept those credit cards. Look for a decal like this:

In those stores, you take your smartphone, tablet or laptop in with you and do your Bitcoin transaction with that particular merchant. Spending Bitcoins is not difficult once you understand how wallets work. We suggest you practice sending very small amounts from your Bitcoin wallet to your receiving address to learn how the process works.

What will have to happen for the average American, Brit, Mexican or anyone to say, "I think I would rather pay in Bitcoin than the dollar, pound, peso" or whatever the local currency is? What will have to occur before people make everyday purchases at markets, restaurants, etc., with Bitcoins stored on their phones instead of local cash?

We are at a tipping point right now. Whenever you have a currency or monetary system, you have to build infrastructure for it. You have to build banks and processing networks. You have to have infrastructure in place for the transactions to occur.

We have infrastructure for the peer-to-peer (person-to-person, person-to-business, or business-to-business) transactions already in place. What is needed now is infrastructure being built at the business level where you can go into a restaurant and pay in Bitcoin. You must have an easy payment platform for being able to pay your check at a restaurant, movie theater or wherever you would like.

That infrastructure is not well-built yet, but it is being built, such as the previously mentioned Bitcoin ATM in Canada and others being ordered, built and shipped around the world.

10 How to Earn or Receive Bitcoins

There are several ways to earn or receive Bitcoins, and one is a method we just got through talking about – accepting Bitcoin as payment for a product or service.

You can earn Bitcoins from mining. You can earn Bitcoins as interest payments. You can earn Bitcoins by getting tips. You can earn Bitcoins as regular income -- people can pay you in Bitcoin. It is not suitable for everyone, but there are plenty of websites that accept Bitcoin for gambling. You can also receive Bitcoins in trade for other currencies or even cryptocurrencies.

We've already discussed earning Bitcoins from mining. When computers mine, what is actually happening is a computer is adding new Bitcoin transactions to the blockchain, which is the list of all Bitcoin transactions all over the world since the beginning of Bitcoin.

If you loan money to someone in any currency, you can make the terms for the loan, along with the interest, to be repaid in Bitcoin. If we are in a rising market, even if the debtor pays you a set number of Bitcoins, it means you make more money in interest. The drawback is a downturn of the Bitcoin market reduces the interest. It's a risky idea in this still-volatile market.

Bitbond.net allows you to borrow Bitcoins and invest in Bitcoin. They say they pay an expected rate of 10 percent. You can read more about it there.

Bitcoin banking is on the horizon. It's just a matter of time. You will be able to bank at those banks with Bitcoin, and they will pay you a fixed rate on your deposits. Some of the exchanges are experimenting with it now. The banks, in theory, could then lend your Bitcoins out. But what if there's a run on the Bitcoin bank and everybody wants their Bitcoins out? Then you could have the same problem that occurs when there is a run on the bank which does not have money on hand to pay out. In the U.S., there is FDIC insurance with the government backing the deposits. That does not exist with Bitcoin, so if there is a run on a Bitcoin bank, then it would be problematic. So there are advantages and disadvantages.

Can you imagine a day when an employer gives an employee an option to receive their pay in local currency or in Bitcoin? It shouldn't matter to the employer. It is the same amount of money. It could possibly be cheaper to pay in Bitcoin than by doing a direct deposit to a bank because of smaller transaction fees.

Money could be sent from the employer's Bitcoin wallet with a small transaction fee. Currently most of the ones available are independent contractor, or "gig," type jobs.

In mid-January 2014, BitPay announced its API for payroll services. We have not tested or evaluated it, but if you are considering Bitcoin as a payroll option for your company, BitPay is a reputable company with which to start your due diligence.

We're not big fans of gambling, particularly online gambling, but there are numerous websites out there where you can gamble with Bitcoin.

And then there is Bitcoin trading. Basically, with trading activity, you are trying to capture the market moves in Bitcoin. The way it works is there are different trading exchanges where you can actually trade Bitcoin.

The way most people are making money -- and in some cases, losing money -- is trading on some of the more well-known exchanges.

The most well-known exchange for all the wrong reasons is Mt. Gox, an exchange that started in Japan.

In March 2014, the Mt. Gox Bitcoin exchange in Tokyo filed for bankruptcy protection, and its chief executive said 850,000 Bitcoins, worth several hundred million dollars, were unaccounted for.

The exchange's CEO Mark Karpeles appeared before Japanese TV news cameras, bowing deeply. He said a weakness in the exchange's systems was behind a massive loss of the virtual currency involving 750,000 Bitcoins from users and 100,000 of the company's own Bitcoins. That would amount to about 7 percent of all Bitcoins mined to that date.

That same month, we met up with a Bitcoin trader who told us he had lost 95 percent of his Bitcoins because he had them in Mt. Gox. He did not tell us how many coins he lost. But there are people the world over who found themselves in a similar position.

As we mentioned in an earlier chapter, the weaknesses and vulnerabilities in the Bitcoin system have occurred when exchanges and other websites created by entrepreneurs, outside the Bitcoin protocol, are not secure enough to handle the hackers.

We have mentioned it a few times before, but Coinbase has stood the test of time and certainly hackers to date.

Wherever there is value, thieves will try to steal that value for themselves. Several of the Bitcoin exchange sites were built in a timeframe when hackers weren't a problem because there wasn't much value in Bitcoin. That's changed, as has the security protocol that Bitcoin processor sites utilize.

The next chapter will address a point Mt. Gox overlooked to an egregious degree – how to keep your Bitcoins secure.

11 How to Make Sure Your Bitcoins are Secure

Security for your Bitcoin wallet shares some similarities to how we take normal security precautions for our real-world wallets. Since your digital wallets are connected to the Internet, there are additional security precautions that must be observed to protect and preserve your Bitcoin. Given the meteoric rise in the value of Bitcoin, cybercriminals have great incentives to create malware or viruses to steal digital wallets.

In the real world, most people do not carry huge amounts of cash in their pockets. We should have the same consideration for a Bitcoin wallet.

There's no reason you cannot possess multiple wallets. In fact, with Armory you can have multiple wallets at the same time.

For example, you can have one wallet for everyday use. You can keep a small amount of coins or fractions of coins in that wallet. Then, you can have a different wallet where you would hold a large chunk of your Bitcoins for safekeeping or perhaps larger scale purchases. You can add different wallets for different purposes, and each wallet can have its own separate password. So if someone steals your everyday-use wallet, your wallet with your larger holdings won't be at risk because it has a different password.

What happens if you accidentally delete your wallet, lose your wallet or your hard drive crashes? If your Bitcoin wallet is on that hard drive, with no backups stored elsewhere, it's just like losing a cash wallet. In fact, in some cases it is worse than losing a cash wallet. When an honest person finds your cash wallet, they can return your wallet with the money. With the Bitcoin wallet, if your hard drive crashes, the Bitcoins stored in it are lost. They can never be recovered. Nothing can be done to retrieve them.

As part of securing your wallet, you need to perform regular backups. These backups need to be encrypted.

There are two ways to encrypt your wallet. The first is to turn on the encryption function in your software Bitcoin wallet program. If you're using the actual Bitcoin-QT software wallet program, there is a menu option you can select to encrypt your wallet. Next, you apply a strong password that only you know. Then it encrypts your wallet, exits out of the program and makes you rerun the program.

Important note, if you have used your wallet before encrypting it: It was receiving transactions before you did the encryption, and you backed those up before you did the encryption. You need to make sure you carefully remove those. It is beyond the scope of this book to teach people how to do this, but we strongly recommend doing an Internet search for directions on how to do this, because you should be very careful before you delete things. You must be certain you do not delete the wallet information.

We also recommend you encrypt your backups, especially if you are going to put them online, perhaps in the cloud. This is a precaution for occasions such as if you have a fire or if someone steals your computer. Then your backups are not stored on the computer at your home and/or business.

One of the best features about the Armory software wallet is it has the ability to print out a page that contains all of the wallet information needed to restore your wallet. In the event your computer crashes or your computer is stolen, you are secure. You have encrypted all the information. You are protected, as long as people do not know your password to connect it to your wallet.

With this paper backup, you can retype the wallet information from Armory and reload it on your new or repaired computer. You key in the codes on the paper. It is not difficult to do at all.

Once you've done that, you can allow Armory to reset itself. It first needs to re-download the blockchain, which can take anywhere between 4 to 48 hours, depending upon your Internet connection. The blockchain grows every day, so it will take longer as time progresses. (Again, the blockchain contains every single transaction that has occurred since day one of the Bitcoin.)

The reinstall will recover all the transactions prior to the computer crash to make sure you have the proper Bitcoin balance for that particular wallet. If you are doing print backups using Armory, then you would need to print out backups for each one of your wallets. It's a very cool feature. It allows you to keep your backups in a secure location like a safety deposit box, a safe or a third party.

As part of the restoration process, you need to know the password. With it, you can recover the coins. We have multiple wallets, have them printed out on paper, and store them at an offsite location.

You should never, ever forget your password. You must be able to remember it, or where you have stored it, even after years of not using it. You may have a wallet where there are still coins inside, and you can't remember the password. If you don't know it, then you are out of luck. There is no password recovery link like you see on most websites that require passwords. Your coins are forever lost.

Always use a strong password. You need to have a password that contains letters, numbers, punctuation symbols and it should be at least 16 characters long. The most secure passwords are ones generated by computer programs specifically designed for that purpose. And, strong passwords are harder to remember, so it takes effort to memorize them.

Always keep your Bitcoin wallet software up to date. All cryptocurrency wallets are updated over time. Make sure your wallet software is up to date, and follow the instructions on updating so you do not inadvertently delete your wallet. Make backups before updating!

Online web wallets are convenient. People may perceive them as being safer because they are not stored on your local computer. Many people perceive the online wallet is more secure because they have a chance to access their Bitcoins even if their computer is stolen. In some cases it might be, but you really are at the mercy of the owner of the company your wallet is with, along with its IT people. So keeping large numbers of coins in the cloud has risks.

Breaches have occurred, and people have lost their Bitcoins. We recommend online storage of Bitcoins only as a temporary option for moving coins around – for example, for temporary storage or for small amounts you might use for a transaction away from your home computer.

It is similar to having a bank account in a city other than the one you live in because it is more convenient to use that bank.

Be sure to do your due diligence on any companies you are using to see if they have been breached before. Also, make sure they have two-factor authentication. (An in-depth description of what that means is beyond the scope of the book, but make sure they have it, you turn it on, and you are using it.)

With online wallets, you cannot control the encryption, but you can control your own password. So make sure you use strong passwords and never forget them. The online wallets do have a mechanism for e-mailing your login password back to you if you happen to forget it. That creates a security risk, but if you are using two-factor authentication and using it properly, then you must give them that second factor before they mail your password. This helps to ensure they are mailing it to the right person.

Web attacks on all of these sites occur constantly. Various techniques and tactics are used to prevent them, including firewalls and protections that the IT people can use to try to prohibit unwanted intrusion into the networks. There are many known ways to hack websites. The companies that host online wallets and facilitate Bitcoin transactions are doing what they can to help mitigate and keep that from happening.

But just understand it happens. Late in 2013, Adobe and Target were breached, just to name two huge companies with complex computer networks and firewalls. Usernames and passwords were stolen from Adobe, along with people's credit card information, which was also stolen from Target's point-of-purchase credit card terminals.

Adobe admitted the theft to the public and offered a free year of credit monitoring for people to be able to watch their credit report.

Target set up a hotline for consumers who had questions to call. The point is: Don't ever assume there is any computer on the globe that cannot be hacked.

It's best to have a balanced approach. Keep some of your Bitcoins online for commerce, some of your Bitcoins in a wallet on your computer, and some in cold storage. Then make sure your wallets are backed up.

There are computer hackers, spyware and early spyware Trojans (viruses) that actually look for the location of your wallet. The programs would capture the wallets and email them to people who stole the information.

Before you put any Bitcoin in your wallet, make sure you have already gone through the encryption step. If so, you have already defeated the thieves' ability to steal your coins as long as your wallet password hasn't been compromised.

If the hackers have a keylogger installed on your computer, the keylogger records your keystrokes. Then they would have the ability to capture what you are typing. In addition to that, if they have copies of your wallet, then it can be decrypted and the coins sent to another wallet. So make sure you have the latest virus protection programs on your computer. We suggest not storing your passwords online or on the same computer with your wallets. We realize some of this is common sense, but you'd be surprised how many of us don't take such simple precautions.

Then make sure you are not visiting unsavory websites where viruses, Trojans and malware can be automatically installed on your computer. We use Macintosh equipment, which seems to be more secure and more reliable.

Finally, we recommend you do not have all your wallets on one computer. If you are going to hold large amounts of Bitcoins in wallets, you must plan to protect them. Unlike a bank that has a vault and has ways to recover money if it is stolen, we do not have that same luxury with Bitcoin. If wallets are not backed up and encryption is not being utilized, then your Bitcoins are at risk!

So while you can't absolutely prevent theft, you need to take steps to protect yourself against loss by following the steps outlined in this chapter.

12 Bitcoin Goes Viral

The reason Bitcoin exists, stated in simple terms, is there is a need for Bitcoin. With the increase in the Bitcoin price we have seen over the last year, there is a definite demand for it. Because of the demand, it has a great future.

If you look at the rush to market by a lot of the competing cryptocurrencies right now, there is definite interest in the cryptocurrency marketplace in general -- further supporting the case for the existence of Bitcoin.

There is such interest, in fact, that a website launched in January 2014 made it a snap to create your own cryptocurrency for a few fractions of Bitcoin. You could have been dead serious, joking around, or trying to make a sarcastic point with the name you gave your cryptocurrency at Coingen. It was off to a flying start when it launched in January 2014, but by August we could find no signs of the service any longer.

Now the practice of creating new cryptocurrency coins has gone mainstream, with the creation of several ICOs (initial coin offerings). The similarity in the way the name sounds to the more familiar IPO (initial public offering) of stock is no accident. The practice is very similar. Investors are given the opportunity to purchase a newly created cryptocurrency in the hopes that it will eventually increase in value. Most of these endeavors are attempting to leap over thousands of rivals and become one of the dozen or so coins that avid cryptocurrency investors will recognize and purchase.

In July 2017, a company names Tezos raised $232 million worth of Bitcoin and Ethereum in just a few days. Its project has been described as a "self-amending" blockchain, given that one of its central concepts is the ability for network-wide changes to be decided upon at the protocol level by stakeholders. Just like investors in the traditional financial markets, cryptocurrency investors are looking for the next big thing. Whether or not the Tezos coin will fulfill that hope still remains to be seen.

Right now, various governments are studying and formulating opinions about Bitcoin. In July 2017, Japan eliminated a tax on Bitcoin, prompting a huge influx of Japanese investors. A big jump in the value of Bitcoin in July and August 2017 was driven in large part by the demand from Japan.

At the same time, Australia announced it was treating purchases of Bitcoin as a currency exchange instead of a purchase. Therefore, purchases of Bitcoin are no longer being taxed in that country. Eventually, laws will be created in most countries to regulate Bitcoin as an industry.

There are immense amounts of venture capital being invested, which is building the infrastructure for the Bitcoin and cryptocurrency industry.

There are limits on Bitcoin regulation. The movement of coins can't be regulated given how transactions move around peer to peer. But what can be regulated is converting a coin into local currency if such a need exists.

Also, because of the infrastructure being built, we are likely to see processes allowing easier ways to purchase Bitcoin. Companies are in a mad dash to create and distribute Bitcoin ATMs all over the globe. The first one we heard about opened at a bar in Canada in 2013. You can go to the ATM at the Waves Coffee House in Vancouver, British Columbia and convert Canadian dollars into Bitcoin at the terminal. It will print out a piece of paper you can scan and receive your money on your phone.

The sending and receiving addresses are quite long. Addresses contain numerous numbers and characters in them, so it would be very hard for someone to type by hand without making a mistake. You do not want to make a typographical error when sending OR receiving money, because you could potentially send it to the wrong person or send it nowhere. There is no way to recover a lost coin if you make a mistake.

Online Bitcoin exchanges, where you can trade Bitcoin for other fiat currencies and cryptocurrencies, are being built by venture capital money. An example is the ability to link a checking account to a Bitcoin account. It's being developed now.

Very intelligent groups and business people are working on various pieces of the Bitcoin economy. As the ecosystem grows, the Bitcoin economy will become more stable. It is already secure as a platform, but we look forward to it becoming more stable as more people begin to participate in the Bitcoin economy.

We're seeing mainstreaming of Bitcoin and cryptocurrency. All new technology in any marketplace goes through a flat period before it is accepted into the mainstream. Then it has a hyper-growth and a flattening-off period, both of which we saw in late

2013. Hyper-growth resumed in 2016, and with a few respites, continued into 2017. We look for this mainstream interest in and acceptance of Bitcoin to continue to accelerate over the next few years.

The number of coins being minted occurs at a constant rate. The final number of Bitcoins is only going to be 21 million, and we are right now at 12 million to 13 million Bitcoins. So at the current rate of growth, we should mine the last Bitcoin in the year 2040 timeframe.

If the Bitcoin demand continues to increase with a steady yet fixed supply, then Bitcoin price appreciation should continue for the foreseeable future. Don't be concerned about the 21 million Bitcoin limit. Bitcoin is traded in fractions of Bitcoin up to eight decimal places. The name chosen by popular vote on the Bitcoin forum to call the fractional portion of a Bitcoin is a "MilliBit." One thousand (1000) MilliBits refers to one (1) Bitcoin or 40 MilliBits refers to 0.040 Bitcoin.

There are hurdles to face with Bitcoin, including the security risks, the volatility of the Bitcoin price, the acceptance by people to use Bitcoin as a mode of payment, and the ease of purchase and selling of Bitcoins to your local currency. That is, to move in and out of your local currency.

There are other problems, but these are the primary ones. We look for these problematic areas to be addressed either through better education, or with new technology being developed to allow Bitcoins to be purchased and sold in a more rapid fashion.

One of the criticisms right now as we are putting this book together is the sudden surge in Bitcoin interest and price is simply a bubble that will eventually burst. Any time you have a rush of people entering the marketplace and the speculation occurring, that can be a bubble. But as you begin to see the market mature -- with the coin actually being used for commerce -- it is less likely to be a speculative bubble. We are seeing more and more of the coin being used for commerce as it is being accepted by some of the household-name companies we mentioned earlier.

Right now, most people are using Bitcoin for speculative purposes rather than ordinary purchase purposes. So there is a lot of price volatility right now, as we have a shift of people who bought the coins in the early days when they were worth less than they are today, to people who are in the mainstream public who are interested in buying coins for commerce use or for speculative purposes.

It is not a bad thing to have speculation, because it provides liquidity for any market. As new coins are mined, the speculative part of the market creates more liquidity for people using it as commerce to be able to convert it back to the local currency.

When a business owner has a Bitcoin, he or she needs to convert it back to the local currency quickly. Therefore, he or she needs to find someone who is interested in buying the coin to convert that coin to the local currency. If you think the problem all the way through, speculators are a big part of the marketplace to create that liquidity. The speculator is interested in the coin because he hopes the coin is going to go up in value. The business owner needs to convert that coin at that particular moment to the local currency so he or she can run his or her business. So the speculator provides a role in the whole ecosystem or economy.

We've watched the Bitcoin rise from just a few dollars to a peak of $4,600 USD (at the time this version of the book was released) in about eight years, with admittedly much of that spike coming in early 2017. With each jump in price, the media has said we are in a bubble.

The price is very volatile. It does move up and down on a day-to-day – even hour-to-hour and minute-to-minute -- basis. After the peak of $1,200 USD in late 2013, the exchange price gradually slid. One big hit occurred with the aforementioned Mt. Gox loss of Bitcoins and subsequent bankruptcy. In the summer of 2014, Bitcoin prices stabilized in the $600 USD range -- fluctuating as much as $100 either direction from time to time, but nothing like the amazing price fluctuation of late 2013.

It became clear during the very bumpy days of early 2014 that Bitcoin is here to stay. If it was just a lark or bubble, there would have been a panic sale and it all would have been quickly over. But that didn't happen, and that's because there are investors and speculators around the world who understand the best is yet to come for Bitcoin and cryptocurrencies. We look for the price volatility to subside as more and more people use the coin for day-to-day transactions. The true value of Bitcoin will find equilibrium at some point to help make the coin less volatile.

As the major governments and financial management agencies begin to deal with the regulatory issues of cryptocurrencies, look for that to also stabilize prices. Literally, a government can make a pronouncement that can have a very dramatic, positive or negative, impact on cryptocurrency, as we mentioned with the removal of Bitcoin tax in Japan and Australia. One example is the previously mentioned Chinese government announcement in December 2013, when the Chinese government declared they are not going to allow Bitcoin to be used in everyday commerce. They will allow Bitcoins to be used in investing and speculative purposes with the understanding speculation and investing carries inherent risk. Since then, China has emerged as the worldwide leader in the creation of companies using supercomputer farms to mine Bitcoin.

But just because a government makes a pronouncement that you can't use it for day-to-day transactions doesn't mean a society will actually observe it. It's especially true in the nature of cryptocurrencies. They are peer to peer. It is individual to individual and business to business. Because a government makes a statement does not necessarily mean the citizens will follow.

One strike against that happening in China is it is, in effect, a crime to buy products and services with Bitcoin there. It is no different if you and I have a dollar bill in our wallet and we decide we want to go and buy something the government says is currently illegal. If a person is willing to take the risk of getting caught, then they can spend whatever they want. They have the freedom to do that. Yet there might be consequences.

And, in early 2014, the U.S. Internal Revenue Service announced Bitcoin would be considered as a commodity, rather than a currency. While some were deflated by the non-currency announcement, others saw the statement as recognition by the U.S. government of Bitcoin.

Each government is going to have to grapple with how to deal with this without killing it, because Bitcoin is actually a good thing. Cryptocurrencies have merits that governments need to recognize and potentially build into their own currency systems, such as safeguards against rapid inflation. Whether governments will actually do that is left to political discussion, depending upon your persuasion.

Right now, we are trying to discover the true value of Bitcoin. We do that by the price fluctuation, which is why it goes up and down. At some point it should stabilize, much like gold has stabilized.

As more people are shopping online, it is completely within the realm of possibility that companies like mega-retailers such as eBay, Amazon, Walmart, Best Buy and others might accept it.

Bitcoin may become another form of payment, just like MasterCard or Visa. Why would a business owner be interested in that? Well, the transaction fees they have to pay to convert the transaction into their currency are much less. It is only 1 percent, compared to credit card transaction fees of at least two or three times that.

Why is it less? It is a lot harder to commit fraud with Bitcoin. It is much more difficult to steal a Bitcoin than to steal a credit card number.

Other advantages to businesses include the clearing process back to local currency does not take as long. The clearing process to receive money on Visa or MasterCard for a merchant can be 35 days. The clearing process to receive your money with Bitcoin is about two days. The result is that it speeds up cash flow.

So the adoption will be pushed along by more people hearing about Bitcoin's advantages through education and word of mouth. People like you are seeking out books like ours. Bitcoin symbols are beginning to appear on a lot of the websites and stores where Bitcoin is accepted as a form of payment.

13 Keys to Bitcoin's Continued Growth, and How You Can Get Involved

When the genesis block of Bitcoin was mined in January 2009, one wonders what Satoshi Nakamoto's vision was for how Bitcoin would have matured after five years.

Here is the conclusion to the project document he/she/they published in 2008 prior to launch:

"We have proposed a system for electronic transactions without relying on trust. We started with the usual framework of coins made from digital signatures, which provides strong control of ownership, but is incomplete without a way to prevent double-spending. To solve this, we proposed a peer-to-peer network using proof-of-work to record a public history of transactions that quickly becomes computationally impractical for an attacker to change if honest nodes control a majority of CPU power.

"The network is robust in its unstructured simplicity. Nodes work all at once with little coordination. They do not need to be identified, since messages are not routed to any particular place and only need to be delivered on a best effort basis. Nodes can leave and rejoin the network at will, accepting the proof-of-work chain as proof of what happened while they were gone.

"They vote with their CPU [hashing] power, expressing their acceptance of valid blocks by working on extending them and rejecting invalid blocks by refusing to work on them. Any needed rules and incentives can be enforced with this consensus mechanism."

Interestingly, because of the reference to people voting with their CPU power, there seemed to be no anticipation that, in effect, mining supercomputers owned by a select few would be doing the vast majority of mining. People voting with CPU power alone in the Bitcoin world these days basically don't have a vote.

For Bitcoin to flourish as a fully accepted and desired payment alternative, all of these will need to become reality:

1) Some market force will need to drive the Bitcoins from the wallets of the select few with supercomputers who are currently doing the mining, and into the wallets of the average person who can spend them;

2) Some market force will need to drive merchants to demand solutions for them to be able to both accept and then exchange Bitcoin;

3) Some market force, probably entrepreneurs, will need to create systems which make the use and transfer of Bitcoin much easier than it currently is.

Point number one on that list is key, though. With only 21 million Bitcoins ever to be mined, what is going to motivate those who currently hold great numbers of them -- such as the Winklevoss twins (Facebook co-founders) and presumably the mysterious Nakamoto -- to spend or transfer enough of them into general use for there to be a legitimate chance for John Doe or Jane Q. Public to acquire and use them?

This is one of the reasons why currently Bitcoin is seen as primarily an investment vehicle and asset.

But what could motivate the Bitcoin investors to spend it instead of hold it is the savings they can realize on purchases. We have already seen several major retailers begin to accept Bitcoin. We believe if Bitcoin payment processing systems are developed that will allow mega-merchants such as Amazon and Walmart to save two to three percent over what they have to pay to credit card processors by accepting Bitcoin, it could be a major driving force.

And likewise, if you as a consumer can save two or three percent on a major purchase by using Bitcoin, you will be motivated to at least seriously explore how you could make that happen.

So, we believe the entrepreneurs will continue to drive the cryptocurrency markets for the foreseeable future. They understand what the needs are and the potential rewards.

14 How You Can Get Started Now

By now, you may be asking, okay, just how can I get started? There are numerous points of entry in to Bitcoin/cryptocurrency arena, so here are our suggestions, depending on which activity you would like to start with:

Buying or acquiring Bitcoin

Use an online exchange like Coinbase in the USA to buy Bitcoins. Make sure you set up an online wallet or software wallet to receive Bitcoin in a transaction. If you open an account at Coinbase, a wallet will automatically be provided for you.

If you need to understand what the current conversion rate to Bitcoin from your local currency is, go to www.preev.com. Preev is a simple Bitcoin converter that uses average trade volume from multiple Bitcoin markets to give you an average price. It has the ability to convert different currencies to Bitcoin or Bitcoin to different currencies.

You will need to provide your receiving address (from the Bitcoin wallet you set up) to the seller. That person will use that receiving address to send you Bitcoins from his or her wallet.

You'll receive notice from your online wallet or software wallet almost immediately that you've received Bitcoin.

Accept Bitcoin in your business

Many companies are rushing to market with solutions to allow business people to accept Bitcoins as payment. Here are a few you should consider:

BitPay is the best-known among the current companies providing the payment services. BitPay claims more than 30,000 companies and charities are accepting Bitcoin payments through their services.

Coinbase has a merchant integration system as well. Look for the "For merchants" button at the top of the page.

If you have any doubt Bitcoin is gaining in acceptance, consider that Overstock.com announced in late July 2014 they would offer bonuses to their employees in the form of Bitcoin. The bonus recipients have the option of whether to accept Bitcoin or a fiat currency. Overstock was the first big-name retailer to accept Bitcoin, and customers now make about $50,000 worth of purchases using Bitcoin weekly at that company's website.

Bitcoin investing

You can buy Bitcoin to hold as a store-of-value in the hopes that Bitcoin's scarcity and popularity will continue to cause capital appreciation. Follow the steps outlined above in the "Buying or acquiring Bitcoin" breakout section above. Of course, we advise you to do your due diligence and consider all of the points we have outlined here in this book about both the possible upsides and drawbacks involved in Bitcoin investing.

Some industry pundits feel the Bitcoin is still severely undervalued and could eventually be worth tens of thousands of USD per Bitcoin. Wouldn't that be nice?

In 2017, Saxo Bank analyst Kay Van-Petersen said Bitcoin could reach more than $100,000 by 2027. In December 2016, with Bitcoin trading at $754, Van-Petersen predicted that it would surpass $2,000 in 2017.

"This is not a fad, cryptocurrencies are here to stay," Van-Petersen told CNBC in a phone interview.

"There will emerge two to three main ones. Bitcoin will be one of those. And the reason is the first-mover advantage, the scale and the pioneering."

According to a CNBC article, here's how Van-Petersen came up with his price target in 10 years.

"Van-Petersen is assuming cryptocurrencies in general – not just bitcoin – will account for 10 percent of the average daily volumes (ADV) of fiat currency trade in 10 years. Foreign exchange ADV currently stands at just over $5 trillion, according to the Bank for International Settlements.

"Ten percent of $5 trillion is $500 billion. This is the ADV that cryptocurrencies could have. Bitcoin will account for 35 percent of that market share, which would that $175 billion of the $500 billion figure, he said. This would mean that $175 billion worth of bitcoin would be traded every day.

"Also, Van-Petersen then implies that Bitcoin's market capitalization would be ten times the average daily volume, giving a figure of $1.75 trillion for the market cap. ...

"Bitcoin has a limited supply of 21 million which is expected to be reached by the year 2140. In 10 years, the analyst thinks that there will be 17 million Bitcoin in circulation, up from the current 16.3 million figure.

"If the potential 17 million of Bitcoins in supply is divided by the $1.75 trillion market cap estimate, then each Bitcoin would be worth just over $100,000."

Of course, there are many other analysts who predict just the opposite, that Bitcoin price represents a bubble, and there is no real value to the asset. We cite Van-Petersen because he was correct in his call that Bitcoin would jump from the $750 range in December 2016 to more than $2,000 in 2017.

15 Reasons Bitcoin's Value Could Explode – and Soon

You've successfully made it to the end of your introductory journey with Bitcoin. At this point, you know more than 99 percent of the rest of the planet and you are to be congratulated.

But still, you may be pondering exactly how and even if you want to take the plunge, so to speak, and get involved in buying, trading and holding Bitcoin.

We believe Bitcoin will continue to grow as THE major cryptocurrency. As computer geeks continue to figure out how to safely integrate exterior websites into the Bitcoin protocol, there will be fewer and fewer cases of people losing Bitcoin to cyberthieves, such as what happened in the case of Mt. Gox.

As mentioned previously in this book, there are entrepreneurs and investors currently holding hundreds of millions, if not billions, of U.S. dollars' worth of Bitcoin. You don't hear about any of these people cashing out. That's because these people strongly believe the value of a single Bitcoin is going to increase geometrically and far exceed the $4,400 range it reached in mid 2017.

Venture capitalists believe Bitcoin will not only continue to increase in value, but also will become a major form of monetary exchange, and they are working feverishly to make that happen.

Another reason we believe there will be an exponential growth rate in the value of Bitcoin is that most people don't fully understand how truly scarce Bitcoin is. Only 21 million total will be mined, right? But guess what -- even when that last Bitcoin has been mined, there will be vastly fewer than 21 million in circulation.

About 17 million have been mined already, and it is believed anywhere from 25 to 40 percent of them have already been lost either by human error, hardware failure and, of course, tragedies like Mt. Gox.

In the early days, Bitcoins were worthless, and it is quite possible many Bitcoins were lost because people who held them just didn't give a hoot. Early in the Bitcoin game, losing your Bitcoin would be about like losing a gum wrapper -- an inconvenience, but no big deal.

But, if we figure 25 percent of Bitcoins have been lost, and remove the Bitcoins held by the top 100 wallets (ones that are unlikely to trade them because they are very likely hard-core investors), that is only about 10 million Bitcoins in circulation -- out of around 17 million mined.

When these facts eventually hit mainstream and the panic buying sets in, and as people begin to understand how few of the 21 million Bitcoins are actually going to be in circulation, scarcity in a market created by limited supply and increasing demand will ultimately increase the market's value.

Markets behave this way for anything of value. So if the market cap in May 2017 for Bitcoin was $35.1 billion USD, what will it be in the future if just one of these factors begins to influence price?

- What if the adoption rate grows to 10 percent of the world population using Bitcoin?
- What if it is discovered a greater percentage than 25 to 40 percent have been lost?
- What if the citizens of a country or countries with significant GDP start using Bitcoin as a currency?
- What if it becomes the de facto reserve currency and replaces the United States dollar?

Bitcoin believers, many of whom are the people holding the top 100 wallets, are working on ways to make acquisition and trading of Bitcoin easier for the average person. They are also working on making it more secure, to give the average person more confidence they won't be putting their money at risk by holding it in Bitcoin.

Bitcoin was originally envisioned as THE money for the Internet. The number of big-name companies that have vetted and analyzed their risk in Bitcoin, and still decided to trade in it, is evidence that the original vision has merit.

We believe once mega-retailers such as Amazon and Walmart join the club of businesses accepting Bitcoin, the floodgates will open. Those companies will be able to realize a 2 to 3 percent increase in profits because the exchange fees for Bitcoin will be so much less for them than the fees they are paying banks to process credit card payments for them.

Some of the biggest companies on this planet, along with some of the wealthiest investors, all have motivation to see Bitcoin become as mainstream as possible. If you want to know why something is happening or has happened, an old cliché is to "follow the money." No different here.

ABOUT THE AUTHORS

Brett Combs co-founded several independent game development studios and publishers in the 1990s and early 2000s. He is dedicated to exploring ways of using technology to improve life while entertaining. His experiences in commodity and FOREX trading prepared him to see the potential in Bitcoin before most, and his insights were the basis of the book you are reading. Brett lives in Texas. You can reach Brett at brett@bitcoincoaches.com.

Tom Mitsoff is the author of the best-selling Kindle book, "The Web Ranking Manual." He is a veteran journalist and editor who has won numerous awards from journalism organizations in Ohio, Kentucky and Texas for journalistic excellence. He is also an experienced Internet entrepreneur. Tom also lives in Wisconsin with his wife Angela and their trusty dog Skip. You can reach Tom at tom@bitcoincoaches.com.